Favourit
South Cotswol
Book One

18 super short walks with some longer ideas

(see the index and location map inside back cover)

Chosen by members of the South Cotswold RA Group

Edited, designed and mapped by Mike Garner

ISBN 1 901184 79 X

*With six additional walks this is a carefully updated revision of
our very popular "12 Favourite Walks in the South of Gloucestershire"*

We owe our grateful thanks to the many members who have helped in planning, writing and checking this collection of favourite walks, and making numerous suggestions to clarify and enhance the descriptions. We hope you will find the text and maps as reliable as in our previous books.

A team of members have agreed to monitor the routes regularly in the future. This is the **first** edition of Favourite South Cotswold Walks Book One - we plan to show updates at **southcotswoldramblers.org.uk/books**

Changes are always taking place in the countryside, with new and extended buildings, and new field boundaries. Some are welcome, for example the trend to replace stiles with kissing gates. If you notice a large alteration affecting a walk description, please be good enough to report it to us at **southcotswoldramblers.org.uk** and if you think it is likely to prove a serious problem for walkers **do** also report it to Public Rights of Way Office, Gloucestershire CC, Shire Hall, Gloucester, tel 01452 425577 **prow@gloucestershire.gov.uk**

Dedicated to friends no longer able to walk with us

Though walking is inherently one of the safest outdoor activities, no activity is completely without risk and it is your responsibility to behave sensibly and to minimise the potential for accidents to occur. Road walking has been kept to a minimum, but please take great care when crossing or walking along roads.

Printed by B A Hathaway, Old Market, Nailsworth, Stroud GL6 0DU tel: 01453 833675
Distribution by Reardon and Son, Publishers, Cheltenham, Gloucestershire tel: 01242 231800

Introduction

We hope you find this book a great introduction to a lesser known part of the Cotswolds, quite undeservedly so we think. There is a shortage of walks books published specifically for our area, so hopefully we shall continue to fill the gap. Please ask about our other titles.

Don't miss

● The beautiful Slad valley, haunt of Laurie Lee, author of Cider with Rosie

● Painswick, Queen of the Cotswolds

● The Cotswold Way National Trail

● Slimbridge WWT reserve

● Berkeley Castle and the Edward Jenner (conqueror of smallpox) Museum

● Stroud's Five Valleys with a proud heritage of textile mills, steeply wooded hillsides peppered with former workers cottages and many crisscrossing footpaths

● The Thames & Severn and Stroudwater Canals, now being gradually restored

The South Cotswold area

● Experience great scenery, with surprises around nearly every corner and views over to Wales and the Malvern Hills, much of the countryside in the Cotswolds AONB

● Visit peaceful villages with attractive Cotswold stone buildings and field walls

● Walk along paths by streams and rivers, including the widening river Severn

● Stroll over open commons; nature reserves with wild flowers and butterflies

Public Transport

Bus services, correct at time of printing this book, are shown to give you an idea. See **gloucestershire.gov.uk/travel** for latest timetables or ring 01452 425610 (the Gloucestershire CC travel helpline).

Do check up before travelling.

Our Website

Please visit our website at **southcotswoldramblers.org.uk/books**

● Enjoy photos of walks before or after

● See starting point maps and late news

● Link to latest transport information

● Send us comments and digital photos

● Report difficulties for action by us

● Link to websites related to the walks

Food and Drink

We list eating places to help walkers. Ring in advance to check if hoping to eat during a walk, in case of closure. Due to possible changes of ownership we cannot guarantee quality.

Countryside Code

Follow the Countryside Code (website **countrysideaccess.gov.uk** has further details of the new version)

● Be safe, plan ahead, follow signs

● Leave gates and property as found

● Protect plants and animals, and take your litter home

● Keep dogs under close control

● Consider other people

The Ramblers' Association (RA)

If you live locally, do give our friendly group walks a try. We welcome you on 2-3 walks before joining (see programme on website / ask at a library).

Please support the RA, Britain's largest walking charity, wherever you live. Did you realise members of one group can walk with all groups? Our website has information about the RA and how to join it (see **ramblers.org.uk**), or tel. 0207 339 8500. RA Members have worked since 1935 to promote walking and to improve conditions for all who walk in England, Scotland and Wales.

Walk 1   L
5.5 miles / 9 km / 2 h 45 m
Upper Framilode by the Severn and Barrow Hill views   Margaret Taylor

This is a mainly level walk with one small hill, and explores the neck of the Arlingham Peninsula, where the River Severn loops round for nine miles to progress just over one. There are good views to the Forest of Dean and the meanders of the Severn, and distant Cotswold vistas. You could see and perhaps meet some rare breeds en route. Framilode church by the river is worth a visit, with its unusual painted ceiling. The church is decorated with many nautical motifs, and in the graveyard more than one headstone records a drowning. Framilode expanded in 1779 when the Stroudwater Canal opened and formed part of the Thames and Severn Canal. Now Framilode is a tranquil spot.

Start: upper Framilode, parking by river near church, grid ref. SO 750104, or Ship Inn car park just before river if you intend to eat or drink there. **Maps:** Explorer OL14, Landranger 162, grid ref. SO 751102. **Buses:** no services. **Food and Drink:** The Ship Inn, U. Framilode - 01452 740260.

A　From Framilode Church walk back along road which bends R away from river. After 100 yards turn R at signpost alongside disused canal. Pass houses and back of Ship Inn to road at Saul Bridge and turn R. *(Starting from the Ship Inn car park, walk out the way you drove in and turn R to reach Saul Bridge).* Continue into Saul village *Note the figures of the twin sailors on Dove Cottage, drowned on their first sea voyage in one of six Severn trows (or barges) which sank in a storm in the Irish Sea in 1919. Over the road (No 2 Kitesnest) is a depiction of the captain, also drowned in the disaster.*

B　Near church turn R along a passage between houses opposite Church Lane. Cross stile and bear L along field edge to metal gate. Continue to remains of iron gate near derelict shed. Go ahead with lake on L to a stile; over this and slightly R to walk between the left hand somewhat intermittent avenue of trees to a gate on to main road. Turn R carefully along road until you see a stile and gate on L. Cross field with hedge on L and cross stile to reach river bank. Turn R following Severn Way to enjoy wide

views. After double stile turn R away from river and over 2 more stiles to road. Go R to Fretherne Church, with its decorated spire. Turn L into a lane signed to Framilode as far as the telephone box.

C　Turn L over stile by gate. Follow direction of sign up field, past hollow on R, to metal farm gate. Walk up second field (pylon in distance) skirting plantation on L. At fence turn L by seat over stile. At hedge turn R over stile in horse jump. Following yellow waymark go up bearing slightly to R of three large trees, then over brow. Drop downhill to stile in horse jump a few yards to R of a water trough. Continue in same direction (waymarked) through two metal kissing gates. Turn L along track to join road.

D　Turn R along road and just past a house on R called "Horseshoe Rise" look for FP sign on R. Go R through gate and uphill via garden gate and over stile to ancient oak tree on top of Barrow Hill (203 feet). There are good views from the top. *(You may wish to take a permissive path over the fence by the tree to the trig. point for views of the wide sweep of the River Severn. On a clear day you might see Gloucester Cathedral and the*

Malvern Hills, and the decorated spire of Fretherne Church should be easy to spot. Return, cross fencing and turn R).

E   Continue downhill, then over a stile, keeping wood on L. At bottom of wood turn L over stile. Go through edge of wood, over another stile into field. Cross field to wooden kissing gate. Go through and look for a small metal gate a little way along the R hand hedge. Go through, and walk ahead between hedge and ancient tree, then pass through a gate in L hand hedge a few yards before corner. Cross field diagonally R aiming for gate this side of half-way along hedge. Go through gate keeping hedge on L and

look for double stile 100 yards before end of field. Turn L over this. Go through paddock to metal gate and continue to stile. Cross stile and pass by house and through iron gate to reach road at Priding.

F   Turn R along road by the river. Turn L at "No Through Road" sign between houses, then through a small metal gate bearing a "Public Footpath" notice. Go through gate to follow path close to the river, although depending on the state of the bank you may be forced to divert over stiles along the parallel but higher field path. Emerge into lane to go past or visit the little church of St Peter, Framilode, with its salmon weathervane.

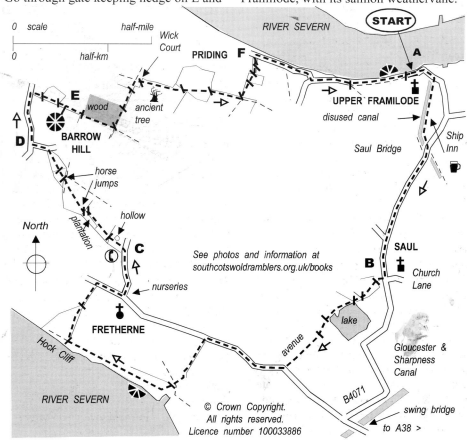

5

Views galore on this walk from Stonehouse as it climbs up over wooded Doverow Hill, then through fields overlooking Stroud and its surrounding hills. Peaceful Randwick Church is reached and good paths are taken through delightful Randwick Woods and Standish Wood. The walk emerges to obtain a panoramic view over the vale to fair Sabrina (as the Romans called the Severn) and to May Hill and the Forest of Dean beyond. Quite energetic, but we think well worth it!

Start: At the back of the main car park in Stonehouse High Street. (charge Mon-Sat). **Maps:** Explorer 179, Landranger 162, grid ref. SO 806055. **Buses:** Monday - Saturday hourly from Stroud (14), Gloucester (14), Dursley (20). Sunday 4 journeys from Stroud and Gloucester (14).
Food and Drink: The Woolpack Inn, Stonehouse (set back opposite the post office in the main street) - 01453 822542, The Vine Tree Inn, Randwick - 01453 763748.

A   Starting at back of Stonehouse car park and facing the railway embankment, turn L along path and ascend steps to railway crossing. Cross carefully and descend steps and over stile into a recreation field. Cross between L boundary and play equipment to a path up between the buildings opposite. Follow this to the road. Do a dog-leg R then L to take a path between houses leading to another road. Turn L for a short distance.

B   At end of road pass through metal barriers and turn R up path between two fences to a stile which leads on to Doverow Hill. Ascend this passing bench near large tree to go through kissing gate. Bear L and take the R of two more kissing gates into Doverow Woods. Take lower waymarked path through woods, passing a kissing gate on R to climb steps. Go forward along edge of hill to another bench, which at certain seasons may give you a chance to survey the Cotswold escarpment and the distinctive flat-topped outlier, Cam Long Down. Leave woods by another kissing gate for good views of hills around Stroud and on a clear day the Malvern Hills on L. Go straight on descending the field to a hedge, passing

two telegraph posts on L. Do not go over stile but turn L along hedge leading to a stile and gate.

C   Follow yellow arrow with acorn symbol (Cotswold Way National Trail) straight up next two fields to stone stile on to road. Turn R for short distance and then follow Cotswold Way signpost L up from road. Go up to stile into field. Climb field and go through kissing gate. Turn R straight along field boundary until it veers away, then head for double gate. Go over iron fence on L into lane and immediately take a R-L dog-leg across on to path again. Pass through gap on L side of gate to continue in same direction and over two stiles to reach a lane. Cross and continue on track opposite, passing to left of metal gate. Look for stile ahead on R of track. This leads you behind the Old Vicarage to a road. Climb a short way to Randwick Church, a peaceful spot.

D   Turn R to go through churchyard and school playground. There are wide views over the Stroud Valleys from here. Turn L up road and after a few yards go up walled path on R. Bear L upwards and follow path as it starts to level out, wiggling R and L and leading to main hill with Vine Tree Inn just down on the L. Continue the walk by turning R uphill for 70 yards and go L through kissing gate. In field go through gap stile and kissing gate into Randwick Woods. Take main path on L which after 150 yards starts to rise. In another 120 yards take the R fork upwards, passing signs Randwick 2000 Steps No 6 and a little further uphill No 7. Continue over track to reach a gap onto another track with multi-arrowed waymarks (The Cotswold Way). Bear half L (yellow arrow) over track onto a good path. After a few yards fork R downhill. Later you have a choice of two parallel paths down to reach wide track. Turn L to pass by R side of wooden gate and soon reach a broad level track.

E Bear L along the broad level track. Pass to the L of a vehicle barrier and then through gap on R of a metal gate. Continue on to cross stile by a huge stone. Cross the field. (The lone Randwick Ash on skyline up on L can be seen for miles. Doverow Hill may be spotted straight ahead). Step through stile by gate to turn R down sunken bridleway. Go through gate and R downhill to Standish sign. Bear L down a track to reach a lane with wide views and follow

this down past Moreton Hill Farm Care Centre until it levels.

F Turn L (signposted Stonehouse 1 km) and just before Maidenhill Lodge, cross stile by gate into field. Cross to middle of far hedge by trees with playing fields on R to a stile in the middle of the hedge. In next field keep to R hand boundary. Go over three stiles through two paddocks and an enclosed path to road. Turn L then bear R round Cotswold Green keeping R on lower road where it divides. At end turn R down an enclosed path and follow it round until it opens out. Turn R down a short road of bungalows (named Bramble Lane at bottom). Now turn L (Meadow Road), then bear L along Paddock Rise. Opposite Kestrel Court turn R down path, and retrace your steps over recreation field, back to railway crossing and car park.

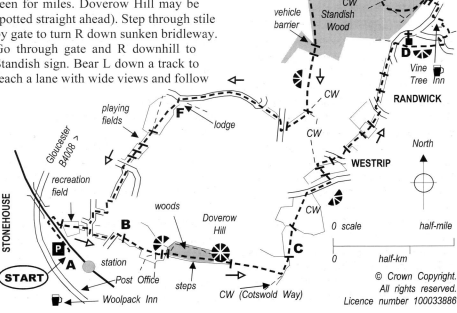

7

This walk starts in the picturesque village of Painswick. There is an interesting lychgate to the churchyard with its famous yew trees, and stocks just outside at the rear. Painswick has many 16th century buildings and its narrow streets provide fascinating views of these. The walk follows the Painswick stream and passes several old mill buildings. It climbs to Pitchcombe and after visiting this lovely village a further climb is made to Pitchcombe Wood. The path around the edge affords superb views. From Edge Common a descent is made to cross the Washbrook, then tracks and field paths are taken to climb back up to Painswick.

Start: Painswick, Stamages Lane Car Park (charge Mon-Sat), grid ref. SO 865095 or Edgemoor Inn, Edge SO 850090, point E, if patronising the pub. **Maps:** Explorer 179, Landranger 162.
Buses: No 46 from Nailsworth, Stroud, Cheltenham hourly Mon - Sat & a few on Sundays.
Food and Drink: The Edgemoor Inn, Edge - 01452 813576, The Falcon Inn, Painswick - 01452 814222, The Royal Oak, Painswick - 01452 813129, or cafés in Painswick.

A From the car park, turn L down Stamages Lane, going straight ahead over crossroads until the stream is reached in the valley bottom. A squeeze stile on the R leads over two more stiles by the stream into fields. Follow stream straight ahead to footbridge over sluice alongside the attractive King's Mill. Turn L at the end of the bridge, and follow the track around the grounds of the mill, ascending a track to join another coming in from the L. Carry straight forward to go between Sheephouse and Dovecote Cottage.

B Keep straight on through a kissing gate and ahead over the field to a stile. Go down the slope almost half L, cross the stream by footbridge and climb half R to a stile. Cross the stile and turn half R until you see a stile in fence to R of large tree. Head down towards lower house crossing two more stiles with the house on your R. After a few yards turn R down enclosed steps to emerge onto lane and turn R. Look out for some preserved mill machinery in the garden (on the R). Walk 100 yards along lane turn L over stile leading uphill past an electricity pole. At the top look for a gate and a stile to the A46. Walk a few yards L until you see a stile opposite. Cross the road carefully and once over the stile climb steeply up the field to find another stile in top L corner by a house. A path leads to the road. *(Pitchcombe Church is a few yards uphill if you wish to visit).*

C Cross the road and take minor one ahead into Pitchcombe village. There are many styles of building to be enjoyed along this road, with fascinating glimpses through hedges and down alleyways. The road goes down then steeply uphill, where there are excellent views back. At crossroads turn R and continue up along short road to a gate into field. Go up field with hedge on R until gateway is reached. Turn R along to gate and stile and then follow the path just inside wood to another gate. Continue round the edge of the wood for nearly a mile. Near the end pass five bar metal railings on R to reach a gate. Go through into a field overlooking Resthaven Care Home.

D Follow wall on L up to the end of the wood and then turn R down field edge to stile in corner. The path ahead leads down to the drive to Resthaven. Turn L along drive, and where it turns R downhill, continue ahead up track for quarter of mile onto Edge Common. Cross open area to silver birch trees. Turn sharp R by Cotswold Way marker downhill to reach a gate onto road. *(You will now follow the National Trail acorn signs all the way to Painswick).*

E **[Alternative Start]** Cross road by Edgemoor Inn very carefully, turn R and then L down minor road, Jenkins Lane. In quarter of mile go L through kissing gate and go ahead to pair of gates on R. Go through both downhill, passing Cotswold Way stone with inscription Chipping Campden 47, through gate to footbridge. The path rises through small wood, through gate into field to emerge on to track on L by means of yet another gate. Go R down track and turn R to pass in

front of Washbrook Farm. There is some interesting stone carving on its wall.

F Go through gate and uphill via another gate to emerge into field. Keep hedge on L at first and then cross the field in same direction until you reach kissing gate in hedge. Ignore this and go slightly uphill to next gate. Go through this and follow fence on L uphill. Go through gate to walk between gardens. Ignore road ahead and turn R on enclosed path. Go through gate and follow fence on R through Hambutts Field. At road turn R over stile or through kissing gate and you will soon see the half-timbered lychgate of Painswick Church. At the junction turn L to explore Painswick, or turn R downhill to reach car park on L.

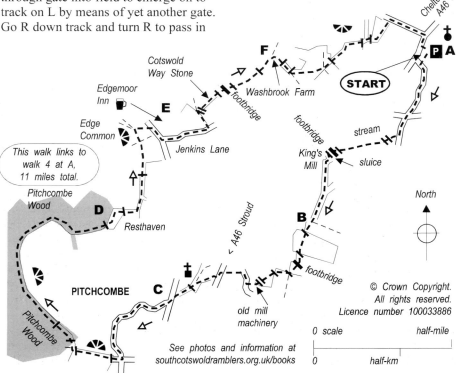

See photos and information at
southcotswoldramblers.org.uk/books

9

Walk 4   M   Painswick, Sheepscombe and the Painswick Stream   Brian Kirkman

6 miles / 9.5 km / 3 hours

This walk also starts in Painswick, sometimes called "The Queen of the Cotswolds". It visits the small delightful village of Sheepscombe. There are several hills, but with the reward of fine views of the valley and the unmistakable spire of Painswick Church. Above Sheepscombe an open area is home to pyramid orchids, in flower in the summer. The route goes through woods, a lovely garden, and descends to the Painswick Stream. This is followed back to Painswick and the walk passes the Royal Oak pub and through the churchyard with its yew trees to the start point.

Start: Painswick, Stamages Lane Car Park (charge Mon-Sat), or park on A46 outside car park.
Maps: Explorer 179, Landranger 162, grid ref. SO 865095.
Buses: No 46 from Nailsworth, Stroud, Cheltenham hourly Mon - Sat & a few on Sundays.
Food and Drink: The Butchers Arms, Sheepscombe - 01452 812113, The Royal Oak, Painswick - 01452 813129, The Falcon Inn, Painswick - 01452 814222.

A   Go to car park entrance and turn L down Stamages Lane. After about 150 yards by signpost turn L through gate on grassy walk with wide views. Continue to end noting memorial stone. Go through gate to end of drive. Turn R down Knapp Lane. At R hand bend, take footpath directly down to Kingsmill Lane. Cross lane and continue past Painswick Mill with pond on L. Here road bears R and also changes to a track. At top opposite a gate turn sharp L. Several gates and stiles will be met along path. Go past stables on R to meet tarmac drive. At end is road. Here bear L and immediately R onto another drive (Brook Farm) with stream on L. Keep straight on over two stiles. A set of steps leads to third stile. Go over and turn L along wall. You might notice the grave of a Polish airman in the grounds of Lovedays Mill. Cross stile in corner of field.

B   Turn R steeply uphill, following hedge. Continue up over stile by gate to reach bungalow. To R of this is a Quaker Burial Ground (and can be visited). Turn R to pass Dell Farm. Continue up rough track for about 200 yards. Look for gate, stile and waymark on L. Cross and continue with hedge on R to gate. Cross open field in same direction to a SP. Turn R up road and shortly fork L. Continue along road, keeping L at further road junction. After about 400 yards, look for a bridleway sign on the L by Pyll (or Pill) House. Go down drive bearing R and pass between houses to go through two gates. Continue along field with hedge on R to old gate. Go through and bear half L to continue along field boundary to stile. Over this bear L downhill to stream. Cross footbridge and stile, and climb up following power line. Aim for double gates at top of hill. The drive leads to road, where turn R. In 100 yards is the Butchers Arms. **[Walk 5 might be followed from here, C]**

C   If not stopping at the pub, turn up a small steep road before it (to the L of the front door). The road becomes a track and emerges onto the open hillside. Continue under the power line and climb straight up. Near the top, just before a metal gate turn L. After 50 yards you may wish to pause at a bench on L; a great picnic stop with stunning views. In June and July this area is covered in pyramid orchids. Enter woodland and pass the sign to "Lord's and Lady's Wood". Ignore a path down L after a few yards, and continue up for about 250 yards, to bear L onto a fairly level path. Just after another path filters in from L, at path crossroads, turn L downhill to gate and stile passing rear of another name sign to wood. Bear R onto a lovely level path. 200 yards along, benches have been erected for enjoying the views. Continue and just before meeting a gate seemingly blocking the way, filter to the L and go through a small gate into a garden (Trench Hill). Pass the house on L, and go down drive through gate onto road.

D　　Turn R and at fork in road turn L down waymarked track and into field. Aim for gap in hedge ahead and in second field keep barns on R to go down to a gate by stream. Cross footbridge and turn L, passing house on R. Immediately turn L onto a footpath to soon cross

stream via stepping stones near Olivers Mill ruins. Walk along path with stream on R. Go through three fields and over stile. Cross road to footpath opposite. Damsell's Mill is on R. Go onwards with stream still on R to junction of paths. Turn R over wide bridge and continue, bearing L in line with hedge. Go through gate and on to gate/stile by house (Highgrove). Walk along drive, and where it bears R, go straight ahead over a double stile into field. Pass old tree stump and soon go between a large and small copse. Cross stream and turn R, heading to R of house chimneys on skyline. Go steeply uphill to stile in corner of field. Turn L onto track. Meet village road passing Verlands on L. Continue up road to pass Royal Oak on L, and through churchyard ahead, then L through lych gate and downhill to start.

This walk links to walk 3 at A, 11 miles total.

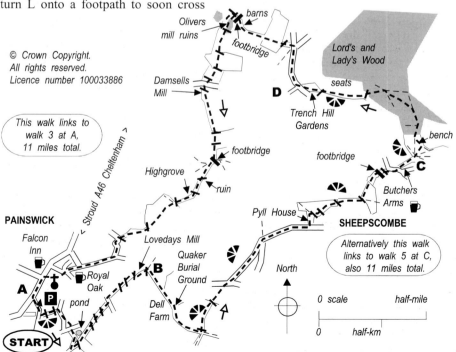

Olivers mill ruins

barns

footbridge

Lord's and Lady's Wood

Damsells Mill

seats

D

Trench Hill Gardens

bench

Stroud A46 Cheltenham

footbridge

footbridge

C

Highgrove

ruin

Butchers Arms

Pyll House

PAINSWICK

SHEEPSCOMBE

Falcon Inn

Lovedays Mill

Alternatively this walk links to walk 5 at C, also 11 miles total.

Royal Oak

Quaker Burial Ground

North

A

P

pond

Dell Farm

0 scale　　half-mile

START

0　　half-km

This walk goes downhill, sometimes fairly steeply through woods and fields to visit the fascinating village of Sheepscombe. A short uphill section takes you to a vantage point overlooking the village, before descending to Far End and into National Trust woodland of high nature conservation value. The bridleway ascends gently most of the way, and shortly before leaving the Ebworth Estate climbs more sharply to reach Foston's Ash, up on the plateau with wide views. Later the route skirts the Whiteway Colony, founded in 1898 by a Tolstoyan anarchist group, and which developed into a patchwork of smallholdings with people living in a variety of homemade sheds, huts, houses and railway carriages etc. In 1924 a colony hall was erected to house social activities and a school house and in 1969 the colony swimming pool was opened. They are the longest surviving secular community in the country.

Start: Park in the lay-by on the L of the B4070 Stroud - Birdlip road, 100 yards past Bidfield Farm / Barns (on the R), grid ref. SO 907106. If you miss parking place (easily done), and find you have reached Foston's Ash Inn, turn round and retrace your route for just over half a mile to Bidfield Farm. **Alternative start points** could be the Foston's Ash Inn, or The Butchers Arms in Sheepscombe (extremely limited parking) but permission of the licensee must be obtained if you wish to park in either spot. **Maps:** Explorer 179, Landranger 163. **Buses:** No 23 Once a week on Thursdays 08:50 from Stroud to Sheepscombe, returning 14:34. **Food and Drink:** Foston's Ash Inn - 01452 863262, or The Butchers Arms, Sheepscombe - 01452 812113.

A   Walk in the direction of Stroud on the B4070 road, keeping on the verge wherever possible, as there may be fast moving traffic. In 250 yards after the barns fork R on to footpath downhill to go over a stile by a steel gate. Continue in the same direction down through a belt of trees towards a stile in the L hand corner of the woods. Enter over the stile and turn L along the path on edge of wood. Look for occasional yellow footpath arrows painted on trees. After 350 yards the path turns R on a waymarked path downhill, crossing two tracks to reach bottom of wood. On edge of wood there is a notice about "Workmans Wood" and a stile.

B   Sheepscombe lies before you with Painswick Church in the distance. Continue downhill across field to a stile just to L of a house. Cross the stream by the footbridge, through a gate, then walk alongside stream via a stile, gate, gap and stile in quick succession. Now cross a paddock to a stile, then go half left down enclosed path to road. Turn R and R again to go uphill. Road soon bears L down again past "Old Stores" on L to T-junction. Go R up wider road to pub.

[Walk 4 might be followed from here, C]

C   [Alternative Start] Facing the Butchers Arms in Sheepscombe, continue L and look for a narrow road up behind it. Climb this, passing Steepways and continue up through wood to reach a junction of paths in the open. Turn R under power line on a level path, noting aerial views over the village. This path later descends gradually to another one in the wood. Turn L uphill for a few yards, then go down clear track to reach road. Bear L past the red post box along the road to Far End. Proceed along the private road between two stone pillars. Follow the blue bridleway arrows and enter National Nature Reserve, also signed National Trust, Workmans Wood. The road now becomes a woodland track through ash and beechwoods. Watch for blue arrows on trees, especially where the route diverges. Pass two man-made ponds on the R of the track. On the L shortly afterwards is a black open shelter showing the work of the National Trust and the Ebworth Estate, and how Workmans Wood acquired its name. Continue up the track leaving the wood through a large timber gate. The bank on the R provides a wonderful display of limestone orchids and wild flowers in season. Pass through a further large wooden gate, then through a small gate ahead to B4070 road. Turn R along footpath on verge. Cross road carefully 100 yards before Foston's Ash Inn.

D [**Alternative Start**] From Foston's Ash continue with care along L fork

signposted Miserden. Turn L at the road sign to Whiteway and then fork L at the bridleway signpost just beyond Wateredge Farm building. Walk along the edge of fields with the boundary on your R. At wood go through the gate on the R, following yellow arrows on trees. After a few yards fork R uphill. Continue into field with boundary on the R. At the top corner turn R over a stile onto a path skirting Whiteway Colony. This develops into a track with bungalows on L. Where track turns L continue straight on using enclosed path and later drive to road.

E Cross road to bridleway which is ahead and slightly to the R. Walk along field with hedge on L to meet road. Cross and go through steel gate and continue ahead. In 350 yards near Bidfield Farm go through small metal gate on R, then the path follows fence around to another gate on to B4070 road. Either turn R back to your car, or turn L to continue walk if you started at one of the pubs.

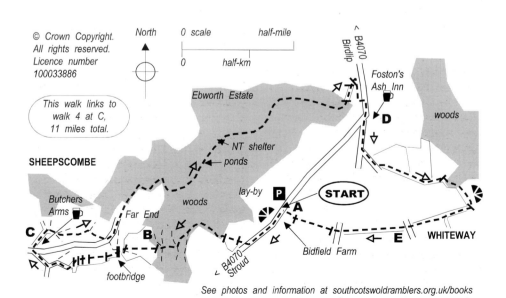

This walk links to walk 4 at C, 11 miles total.

North

0 scale   half-mile

0   half-km

Ebworth Estate

SHEEPSCOMBE

NT shelter
ponds

Butchers Arms

Far End

woods

lay-by   P   START

C   B   woods

footbridge   B4070 Stroud

Bidfield Farm

Birdlip   B4070

Foston's Ash Inn

D   woods

WHITEWAY

E

See photos and information at southcotswoldramblers.org.uk/books

The climb to Coaley Peak Viewpoint is well worth it, as views on clear days are stupendous over the Severn Vale to the Forest of Dean, Malvern Hills and the Welsh Mountains. The return route over fields also has very extensive views. Leonard Stanley is a charming village dating back to Saxon times, with many historical buildings. The parish church of St. Swithun was built in 1129 as a monastery church, part of the Priory of St. Leonard. It has a very solid looking tower and a richly decorated Norman doorway. The former tythe barn is still in use next door in the farm.

Start: Leonard Stanley Church, grid ref. SO 802033. From Junction 13 of M5 take A419 towards Stroud. After 2 miles turn R at traffic lights towards King's Stanley. Go through to Leonard Stanley. Turn L up "The Street" to war memorial and church just beyond. Please park considerately in village. **Alternative start:** Coaley Peak Viewpoint off B4066 Stroud - Dursley, grid ref. SO 794014. **Maps:** Explorer 168, Landranger 162. **Buses:** Monday - Saturday No 14 Stroud, Stonehouse, Gloucester hourly, four on Sundays. **Food and Drink:** Picnic with views at Coaley Peak or do a 15 minute detour to the Rose and Crown, Nympsfield - 01453 860240.

A Facing the church turn L along Gypsy Lane and follow until tarmac ends and the route becomes a bridleway. It develops into a steep stony cutting. *Difficult to believe now but in 1934 a motor car hill climb event was held here which attracted 157 competitors.*

B At the top of the cutting meet a wide track in the woods. Turn R here and continue upwards to a cross roads in the track. Bear R along the Cotswold Way to a gate. Follow Cotswold Way signs. Go up steps which skirt an old quarry. Emerge from woods into a grassy area. In a short distance notice Nympsfield Long Barrow on the R. You are at Coaley Peak. Continue until you see a car parking area on the L. The adjacent area is a very good picnic spot. **PL - Optional Pub Lunch** *at the Rose and Crown, Nympsfield - an extra half mile (15 minutes) detour each way -* **Please ignore this section if not visiting the pub.** *Continue past car parking on your L to gate in top L hand corner of field, and after another gate go on to road. Almost opposite is a stile into field. Go ahead keeping hedge on your R*

to a gateway. Go through here into next field and with hedge now on your L continue along to gateway out onto road then turn L to junction where turn R along to pub. Afterwards retrace your steps to the picnic area.

C **[Alternative start]** From Coaley Peak picnic spot walk along edge to gate in far R corner of field. Through kissing gate turn R (down and up hollows) to topograph overlooking the Severn Vale. After taking in the views rejoin Cotswold Way to follow path leading to a kissing gate into a wooded area. Pass old quarry face on L and continue until path climbs steps out onto a busy road - **beware of traffic.** Turn L and go uphill to the cross roads. Follow slip road to R. Noting the Cotswold Way signs, go down through the woods. Leave the Cotswold Way where path forks and take R bridleway downhill to reach a road.

D Continue downhill on this road (Knapp Lane) until it bears sharp L. On the R take the R hand footpath through a gate into field. Bear R of large tree in middle to a stile. Cross to go between two fences, ignoring stile on L, to a stile ahead. Bear L and go level with fence on your R to a farm gate and a few small trees. Continue with fence / hedge on L. The path becomes sunken and reaches a gate. Follow track beyond gate to a road.

E Cross the road and follow bridleway to a gate alongside cattle grid. This leads into a garden. Bear R up drive past the houses to reach a steel gate into field. Go half L down the valley for about 400 yards until you see a water trough by L boundary. Now head half R uphill keeping bushes on your R. Reach a faint track leading to a double gate out onto a very busy road. **Great care needed here.** Cross and walk down the road to a sharp L hand bend. Here escape from the traffic, turning R up a side road leading to Hill Farm Cottage.

F At a meeting point of several paths go into the field, and continue in a similar direction. This takes you down with a hedge on L towards an electricity line. Just before reaching the line, look for a plank footbridge behind a metal gate on L. Cross and turn R, then head for pylon and a double stile by its base. Cross

and walk half L up the slope to another double stile (by tree). Cross and continue slightly L of hump to a stile in the hedge. Cross and turn R. Walk with hedge roughly on your R aiming for a stile. This is a few yards R of gateway in far hedge (near a water trough). Cross stile by brook and then a second stile. Now keep R, following hedge (watch out for badger sett holes) to a footbridge on R. Cross and turn L to go on to a stile and plank bridge. Continue to another plank bridge and stile on the L. Cross next field diagonally to a stile 50 yards to the L of steel gate. Climb stile into Gypsy Lane and turn L to return to the start point at the church.

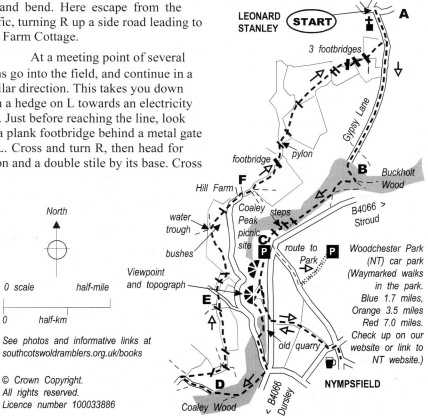

North

0 scale   half-mile

0   half-km

See photos and informative links at
southcotswoldramblers.org.uk/books

LEONARD STANLEY (START) A

3 footbridges

Gypsy Lane

footbridge   pylon

F   B   Buckholt Wood

Hill Farm

water trough   Coaley Peak steps   B4066 > Stroud

picnic site

bushes   C P   route to Park   P   Woodchester Park (NT) car park (Waymarked walks in the park. Blue 1.7 miles, Orange 3.5 miles, Red 7.0 miles. Check up on our website or link to NT website.)

Viewpoint and topograph

E

old quarry   NYMPSFIELD

D   B4066 Dursley

Coaley Wood

15

Woodchester and views from Selsley Common Mike Garner

Try to choose a clear day, as this walk has magnificent views to the River Severn, Forest of Dean, Welsh mountains, Malvern Hills and Marlborough Downs. There is a steady climb through North Woodchester up to Selsley Common, then down across farmland and by the attractive cottages of the conservation area in South Woodchester, and so back across the valley dividing the two halves of the village to the church.

Buses: Monday - Saturday Stroud (46,93,40) every 30 mins, Cheltenham (46) & Gloucester (93) hourly, Wotton-under-Edge (40) 2 hourly. Sunday (46) Stroud/Cheltenham, six all day. Alight at North Woodchester, walk up Selsley Road to follow car route. **Start:** Turn off A46 Stroud - Bath signed North Woodchester, up Selsley Road to telephone box on R. Turn L, then first R. Park on road between St Mary's Church and houses. **Maps:** Explorer 168, Landranger 162, grid ref. SO 840026. **Food and Drink:** Afterwards, walk past upper church gates again and continue along to The Royal Oak, North Woodchester - 01453 872735, or you could stop on the route after 4.5 miles at The Ram Inn, South Woodchester - 01453 873329.

A Follow churchyard boundary up road, then bend R to go past church gates. After 30 yards turn L up drive. When drive bears L to a house, go straight up a path, and after 50 yards turn R up steps with handrail (waymarked). Go along green lane to road. Turn R and go down the road for 70 yards. At Selsley Lodge turn L along a narrow road between stone walls. Shortly after R wall ends, go through a metal squeeze stile on the L into a field. Climb field keeping fence on your L and enter wood over a stile by a gate.

B Follow path gently round to R. When you near the end of wood you have a choice. The right of way forks L steeply up slope and steps to a drive, turns R for 10 yards then goes down more steps into field below house, *or use the very clear level permissive path if still open to avoid steps.* Cross the hillside and go through a copse for 20 yards. Cross a stile, and then go ahead up to a stile in the fence. Cross the next field and aim for an electricity pole between houses and walls. Cross a stile to the L of a pole and emerge on to Selsley Common with Teasel Cottage on

your L. Follow track to cross road, then climb steeply (at almost a right angle to the road) past a wall with conifers, with ascending wall on your R and ignoring sunken track rising half L. Cross a track and climb to a bench. You may wish to rest a while as there are wide views from May Hill to Rodborough. This open area is covered with tracks and hollows from stone quarrying. Keep going up in same direction. Gradually bear L keeping main quarry on your L to reach the top.

C Just before "The Toots", site of a long barrow, is a Millennium Stone Topograph. Weather permitting, enjoy the excellent views, as far as the Sugar Loaf near Abergavenny if you are very lucky. Head across common, aim towards farmhouse and pass fenced top of quarry and pylon to reach road. **[Alternative start point]** Cross to two signposts by another pylon and cattle grid with sign for Bownhill Farm. Walk up drive signposted Inchbrook for 600 yards to a junction.

D Go R over another drive and cross stile. Follow path with wall on your L, noting solitary wind turbine ahead at

Nympsfield. After 200 yards go through metal gate by stile on L. Follow path down two fields with wall and later fence on L. When path bends to R slightly uphill look for slab stile on L 10 yards after passing under power cable. Cross middle of a field following line of power cables to stile in corner. Cross and bear L to cross a slab stile. In third field head to lowest corner, then over stile down through copse to lane. Cross stile opposite and go downhill to gate. Now go down more steps and along level path overlooking Crystal Fountain housing on R and look for kissing gate on L prior to more steps. Go through; climb diagonally to stile in top corner. Turn R along lane. At crossroads turn L up Convent Lane, passing Convent of Poor Clares on R.

E Now look for Atcombe Court Farmhouse on L and after a further 100 yards go L over stile near gate to path with fence on L leading between two ponds. Go through wooden kissing gate and over drive to metal kissing gate. Climb up field and bear L to near top corner by an elegant metal squeeze stile. Turn L, then after 10 yards R. Walk through attractive village until you see a half-timbered house. At crossroads note or visit Ram Inn downhill. **[Alternative start point if using the pub]** Bear L up steep lane, then R up Lagger Lane. In front of last house's garage ahead, turn R down steps to go down through garden, over stile into field, past a marvellous oak tree to stream. Cross footbridge and climb towards church. Go over stile and through kissing gate to finish.

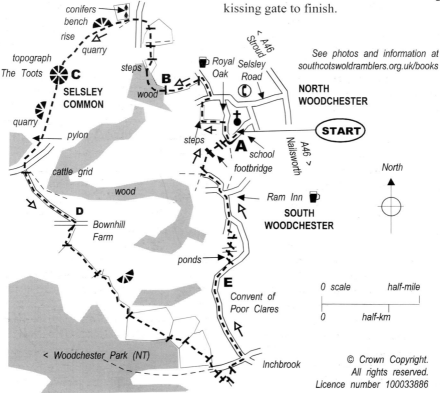

See photos and information at
southcotswoldramblers.org.uk/books

17

Brimscombe, Toadsmoor Valley, Eastcombe, Brownshill
Eric Seymour

This walk heads up the secretive Toadsmoor Valley, passing through the ancient beech woods and by Toadsmoor Pond. Going gradually upwards, it emerges from the woods and climbs more steeply to Eastcombe, with excellent views over the area. At the top of the hill the walk passes through a small part of Bussage to reach Frith Wood. After a pleasant section across the Pleasure Grounds the route descends through Brownshill with its older cottages. The last section downhill is open grassland with views over the Golden Valley to Rodborough Common.

Start: From Stroud take the A419 towards Cirencester for 3 miles to Brimscombe. Just past the turning on the L for Bisley, Bussage and Eastcombe, park in the very large lay-by on the L just before the King and Castle. **Maps:** Explorer 168, Landranger 162, grid ref. SO 877022.

Buses: Monday - Saturday only from Stroud to Brimscombe (54 and 54A) just a few.

Food and Drink: The King and Castle, Brimscombe - 01453 883619.

A   At King and Castle end of large lay-by turn L up steps on signposted narrow footpath. At top turn L along road. At T-junction turn R uphill and near "Eastbourne Lodge" turn L down steps on to narrow surfaced path. Reach main road and do a L-R dog-leg to go steeply up Bourne Lane (signed Quarhouse/Thrupp). Where the road levels and before it goes down again, turn R uphill (signposted Quarhouse). This develops into a country lane. Go straight ahead where road bears up L. Keep "Hillcrest" sign on your R and walk along drive past a stile and old gate posts. The drive starts to slope gently down and there are views over the valley. Keep straight on at stone gate posts. The footpath leaves drive over a stile up to the L of two gates to follow a fenced route. Ignore stile on L. Enter wood at next stile.

B   Follow the main path through the woods. You will pass a fenceless stile. Continue down to small stream. Next comes a longer section with a path joining in from higher up. At fork of two good paths, go R downhill to cross stile on R by metal gate onto lower track. Continue uphill in similar direction. Shortly bear R uphill. Cross another small stream and keep R on edge of wood to descend steeply out of woods past a double garage with circular window. Follow lane steeply up to a T-junction and turn L downhill to reach a ford by bridge over stream.

C   Pass the end of Toadsmoor Pond and turn R to follow the bank, a pleasant place for a pause. Many years ago when there were real winters, fairs were held here on the ice and skating was a popular activity. Continue past the pond and fork R to pass "Keeper's Cottage" on L and more of its extensive gardens on the R. The stream runs through them in a most delightful way and the path continues up the valley with the stream on the R. Eventually path becomes much steeper up to a signpost. Here turn R over a bridge with metal fence to cross the gorge.

D   Follow this track which develops into a surfaced lane going uphill. Fork R very steeply up through trees and round bend to pass "Crows Nest". At five way crossing (sign for Rodways Farm behind you) continue up bearing slightly R to soon pass "Brewers Cottage". Go over wide crossroads, passing church and Eastcombe Village Hall. At top of road turn R and in a few yards look for signpost on L. Cross stile and after a few yards pass another into a road. Bear R to reach a gap and signpost into a surfaced path between houses. This passes school playing fields on R and then you cross a road into a small service road with a green surrounded by houses. Bear L and immediately R to continue in similar direction. Cross a road and pass between houses for just 50 yards. Turn R into Frith Wood. Here there is a bewildering choice of paths. The easiest route to describe is to keep to the R (north) edge of wood, with houses in view on your R. When you spot houses and the end of the wood ahead bear round to L and continue on edge of wood near more houses until you see a single house ahead. Turn R on tarmac path to exit the wood.

E Go forward on this path towards lamp post, and just before it, turn L on an enclosed unsurfaced path leading to the "Pleasure Grounds". Cross, aiming for gap near flagpole. Cross road and go through gate into allotments. At other end bear L along road and turn L at junction. At electricity control box bear R downhill to reach junction at top of Skaiteshill. Turn R on level road. Soon pass

St Raphael's Convent with lovely gardens and continue until reaching wide track on L into farmyard. Dog-leg L and R between buildings to cross stile by metal gate into fields. Pass fenced off pond on R and descend through fields with wide views. Continue through wooden kissing gate to continue down to reach iron kissing gate. Pass through metal squeeze stile and down steps to reach road which leads down to The King and Castle. Turn R to return to start point.

See photos and information at southcotswoldramblers. org.uk/books

Map labels:

D

EASTCOMBE

gorge

Toadsmoor Woods

Keeper's Cottage

C

Toadsmoor Pond

woods

ford

BUSSAGE

stream

Valley

playing field

Toadsmoor

stream

green

E

Frith Wood

woods

Pleasure Grounds

stream

B

allotments

BROWNSHILL

0 scale   half-mile

0   half-km

North

pond

Skaiteshill

St Raphael's Convent

Bisley >

BRIMSCOMBE

START

P

King and Castle

A

< Stroud A419

Cirencester A419 >

19

Cider with Rosie in the Slad Valley
Jim Fern

This is an interesting and varied walk around the beautiful Slad Valley, perhaps the most unspoiled of the valleys converging on Stroud. It has been immortalised by Laurie Lee in his worldwide best-selling book "Cider with Rosie". Although the main route does not enter the village itself, wonderful views can be observed as you pass along the eastern side of the valley and after climbing Swift's Hill you will see an impressive panorama over Stroud and the distant Severn Vale. It is possible to visit the Woolpack Inn and the church 600 yards off the route after point D. The walk is very hilly, but the scenery more than compensates.

Start: From Stroud take the B4070 towards Birdlip for 3 miles passing through Slad village to Bulls Cross, where there is good parking adjacent to the crossroads. A milestone/mounting block on the R marks the start point. **Maps:** Explorer 179, Landranger 162, grid ref. SO 878088. **Buses:** No services to Slad. Ride to Stroud, walk up Slad Road (B4070) 1.5 miles to point D (and 1.5 miles back afterwards). **Food and Drink:** The Woolpack Inn, Slad - 01452 813429.

A   Start from the milestone southwards towards Stroud. After a few yards turn L down a drive to Trillgate Farm. When approaching the farm a hidden stile by a gate on the L leads to a permissive path descending to the infant Slad Brook. Alternatively use the Public Right of Way through the farmyard, turning down L near the dovecote and out into the field through a farm gate. At the bottom go over a stile by gate and keep R up steep field to a gate on to a track. Turn L bearing R at fork to reach a surfaced lane. Turn L and walk up to fork. Bear R signed No Through Road. Follow lane passing Down Court (originally farm cottages) through gate to Snow's Farm. Go over a stile next to gate near farm house and descend half left to small packhorse bridge, many centuries old, crossing the Dillay Brook.

B   Bear R from bridge over stile and enter field. Keep R and approach feeder stream, crossing this on wooden footbridge into another field. Continue across to climb stile into larger steep field. The path is indistinct at first but go half L up towards distant wood. Go through metal gate which comes into view on opposite boundary and follow the path in same direction to a high stile leading into Catswood. Turn R along woodland track until a steel gate across track is reached. Continue on main track and soon go around L bend. Note coming up on the R the ancient sunken route from Painswick to Bisley. After a few more yards fork R downhill, soon admiring views of Slad. Keep on level straight ahead to join a road and bear R. After 200 yards follow signpost L on level track to visit hamlet of Elcombe. At end of track go down by handrail, then turn R down between cottages to reach the road.

C   Turn L and walk along road to cattle grid at bottom of Swift's Hill. Turn sharp L and follow steep track skirting wood on L and passing old quarrying on R. Where the wood ends go ahead to enjoy the views and rest awhile. This is a nature reserve to be respected accordingly. Now follow a clear path down the west side of the hill towards houses to rejoin the road at another cattle grid. Go downhill and turn L and immediately R at the corner junction, signposted The Vatch. Passing early mill cottages hidden on L, continue to corner by beautiful Vatch Cottage on R. Climb stile on R and follow fence on R up a path to go over another stile and up again to the main Slad road. Turn R.

D   [Alternative start for bus users]
From Woodside House on L follow the main road up towards Slad to the end of the wall on L. Look for a signpost on R pointing L. Before turning off note one of the best views of lower Slad village and Swift's Hill. *(If you wish to visit the Woolpack Inn and the churchyard with Laurie Lee's grave, they are a further 600 yards up the road. Then return to this point).* Take the steep surfaced path on L

and through a gate to a track leading to a gate into a field. Keep to path at side of Worgan's Wood on your R to old quarry, and pass over a stile to follow an enclosed path with wood on the R, to reach the ridge road (the original Painswick to Stroud road for many centuries.)

E   Turn R along ridge road passing Worgan's Farm. At T junction of tracks go straight ahead through gap by metal gate onto enclosed path leading into Frith Wood. This is a nature reserve owned by the Gloucestershire Wildlife Trust. At the end of the wood, pass two gates and enjoy the scenery as you cross the common to reach the milestone at the start.

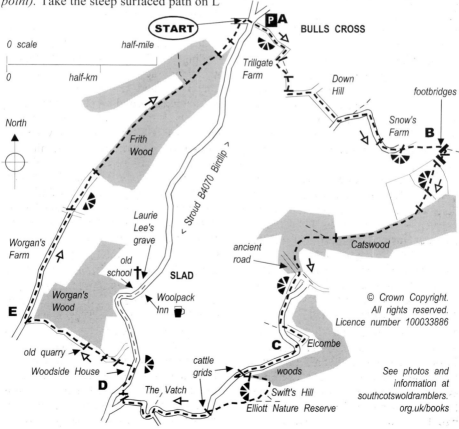

See photos and information at southcotswoldramblers. org.uk/books

21

| Walk 10　　　　　　　M | Sapperton, Pinbury Park, |
| 6.5 miles / 10.5 km / 3 h 15 m | Edgeworth, Daneway　　　Ruth Cook |

Sapperton is a delightful Cotswold village. It was the home for Gimson and the Barnsleys, distinguished members of the Arts and Crafts movement in the Cotswolds. They moved to the village from Pinbury Park, and their gravestones can be seen in the churchyard quite near the top. Formerly the Poet Laureate John Masefield lived at Pinbury. The walk goes through a variety of habitats and is excellent for observing wildlife, including deer if you are quiet. Pinbury Park has glorious views over the Frome Valley. Edgeworth is said to be the most remote village in the Cotswolds and the quiet country later on also has wide views over the plateau. The Thames - Severn Canal towpath at Daneway goes through a Gloucestershire Wildlife Trust nature reserve before reaching the entrance to the two mile canal tunnel. This was the longest in the world at the time of its construction (1784-1789). The walk has two steep climbs.

Start: Park on R side of the "No Through Road" near St. Kenelm's Church, Sapperton. **Maps:** Explorer 168, Landranger 163, grid ref. SO 948034. **Buses:** from Stroud and Cirencester (54, 54A, 28, 28A) are very occasional, Traveline 0870 608 2 608 **traveline.org.uk**

Food and Drink: The Bell Inn, Sapperton - 01285 760298, The Daneway Inn - 01285 760297.

A　　Start from bridleway at telephone box opposite churchyard. Follow fence on L up and go through gate. Turn L and follow enclosed path. Go down through a copse and into field via gate. Cross field until you see track going up to R. When you reach it follow it slightly L down to gate. There is a fine view of Pinbury Park Manor ahead. Go through gate and follow almost level path which soon bends gently to R. Keep fairly level, and aim for small section of wooden fence just below trees on R. Look for large pond. Make for tarred driveway and turn L to go through gate on drive. Continue past two magnificent barns and down by elegant Pinbury Park. Note squirrel and nut topiary on yew hedge and spectacular view. Go downhill on track, ignoring others on R and later on L, to a ford through stream. Bear R to cross stream over wooden footbridge.

B　　Go through gate and cross meadow keeping wood on L to another gate 75 yards away. Continue on path steeply uphill through wood to reach a metal gate. Continue up through two fields with fence on your R to reach a line of trees in hedgerow, "Gloucester Beeches" on the map. Go through metal gate and turn R through small gate. Walk through large field with wall and later fence on R to reach metal gate. Go through two more small fields via gates to overlook peaceful Edgeworth, down in the hollow. In meadow aim for the L of two prominent electricity poles. Keep going and look for gate on R onto road. Follow road for 250 yards through the peaceful village to the old church. The manor house is adjacent (but not open to the public). Pause at the lychgate behind church for wide views. Now retrace your steps along road to gate into meadow.

C　　Head uphill to R, and at top look for gates onto track. Walk to gate leading onto road. Turn L and walk to Edgeworth Polo Club on L. Turn R along drive, passing a long barrow. After half a mile the drive turns away to R. Go ahead through gate and downhill to see a fence/stile in corner. Go over this and walk downhill, keeping boundary on your R. At bottom go over three stepped stile and turn L to cross top of next field.

D Enjoy views. Cross flat footbridge to reach stile in far fence. Follow path to cross a tiny footbridge and walk uphill by tiny stream. Near wooden board fence ahead turn R and go quietly up between buildings of Tunley Farm. In courtyard bear L to walk along a drive. At road continue uphill to turn R at signpost up some steps. Climb quietly up through cottage garden, passing oil tank, to gate. Cross next huge field following fence on R at first. Keep in same direction where field bulges to the R and rejoin hedge

later. Eventually reach stile near gate in far R corner. Head for large fir tree ahead and emerge to see views over Daneway House and to Sapperton. Follow steep path down to R. Go over two stiles. Turn L steeply down to cross a stile onto road. Turn R downhill to reach Daneway Inn.

E **[Alternative Start if using pub]**
From Daneway Inn cross road bridge and turn L through a squeeze stile onto old canal towpath. Follow this through nature reserve, to reach tunnel entrance. Turn L over tunnel portal and cross stile into meadow. Climb up hill to fence on the "donkey path", where horses and donkeys towing the old barges used to climb over summit to reach other tunnel entrance at Coates. Boats were "legged" through the tunnel. Go through kissing gate onto pathway which leads L to lane. Turn L and soon bear L to reach churchyard gate on R. Follow path up through churchyard back to start.

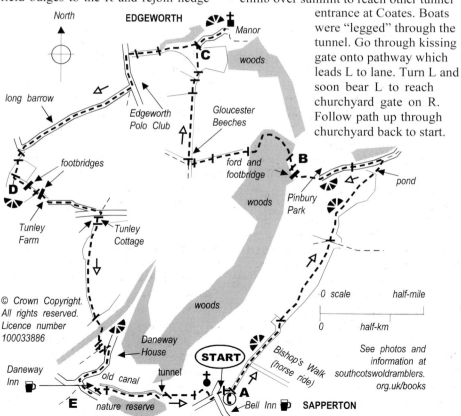

See photos and information at southcotswoldramblers.org.uk/books

Berkeley, Little Avon River, Stone, Whitcliff Deer Park, Ham   Maurice Dyett

Berkeley is historically an old market town with some marine history. The castle traces to before the civil war and has some gruesome tales. In High Street a look at the windows will show how many of the buildings changed use from shops, pubs and workshops. The main sites, castle, butterfly collection, Jenner Museum and church deserve a longer visit. The castle is still home to the Berkeley family, who run the large estate. This walk is generally level with one short steep climb up to the deer park, where there are extensive views. There are at least two breeds of deer in the park.

Start : Berkeley. Leave the A38 on the B4066. Go straight on at the roundabout on outskirts and into Market Place. Turn R at town hall signed Sharpness, and car park (Marybrook Street) is about 200 yards on R, near the Malthouse pub. If full, nearby there is the library car park, and also plenty of on street parking. **Maps:** Explorer 167, Landranger 162, grid ref. ST 684994.
Buses: Village Link VL2 Dursley, VL3 Gloucester, Thornbury, must book on 01452 423598.
Food and Drink: Berkeley Arms - 01453 811177, Malthouse - 01453 511177, Mariners - 01453 811822 , also coffee shop High St, all in Berkeley, and Salutation Inn, Ham - 01453 810284.

A   Turn L from car park, passing hospital, to wide market place. Zig-zag L then R to go along High Street (sign under shop window). Turn L at sign to Jenner Museum. Follow the lane past the museum (The Chantry) and continue into the church yard. The church tower is separate from the church. Turn L at tower along path. Look over museum wall to see thatched roof of the hut where Jenner is said to have worked. Return to the tower. Turn L to visit church or pass church door. Head downhill out of churchyard through gate and turn R (near Castle Gatehouse entrance) to reach main street. Turn L downhill and where the road levels look for a metal gate on L with inbuilt stile.

B   Cross the stile and bear R across meadow, with fine views of the castle on your L. Reach L bank of Little Avon River and follow it upstream. Opposite farm buildings keep on L bank to pass through 3 metal gates close together. Continue through several more fields until you reach an isolated concrete bridge with metal railings. Cross and go along R bank of river into second field. After 150 yards at waymark, turn R uphill to go through gateway. Bear slightly L across open field heading towards R side of clump of trees and old gatepost. Continue slightly R (twin gables in distance a marker) to reach a gateway which comes into view, this leading you onto a quiet road. Turn L along this and soon pass Stone with Woodford school. Turn R along main A38 and bear R into churchyard.

C   At far end of churchyard cross village green and turn R along narrower no through road past large old double gabled house on R. This road leads to Westend House drive. Go along drive and soon path is signed onto L through grounds to reach a stile. Cross this and continue along R edge of field. Where hedge curves to R, continue straight on to far hedge to go through kissing gate. In next field go in similar direction to reach footbridge. Cross and you have a choice of two fields ahead. Go forward through the R one, keeping hedge on your L to reach a stile leading onto road.

D   Enter field opposite and turn R towards bungalow. At gateway turn half

L to cross field to a footbridge in hedge. Cross this and turn R with hedge on R to reach another footbridge. Go across next field with hedge on R to a stile. This leads to a plank across ditch and another stile out into large field. Head across field between two power line poles to reach a plank footbridge. Go across to corner jutting out on R, and continue where field opens up in same direction to reach a footbridge which leads onto road. Go R along road and immediately L into field. Follow L boundary uphill to stile at top. In next field bear R and then L steeply straight up to reach gap in bushes to brick wall of Deer Park. Follow wall around to L and cross two stiles to reach Deer Park entrance over wooden steps on R.

E   Cross Deer Park following white markers for half a mile. On L are great views to the River Severn and Forest of Dean and to R the Cotswold Hills and Stone church. Go through gateway and

on for almost another mile. You may be lucky and spot the herd of deer if you are quiet. At far end the path descends to steps over the wall. Cross these and go down through field to reach the road.

F   Continue along road to pass (or visit) the Salutation Inn at Ham Green. Walk along the road, passing various buildings built by the Berkeley family; cottages, estate offices, stables and kennels. Re-cross the Little Avon River and walk up High Street back into Berkeley. If time look further at church or museum. Continue into the Market Place and retrace your steps to the car park.

See photos and information at southcotswoldramblers.org.uk/books

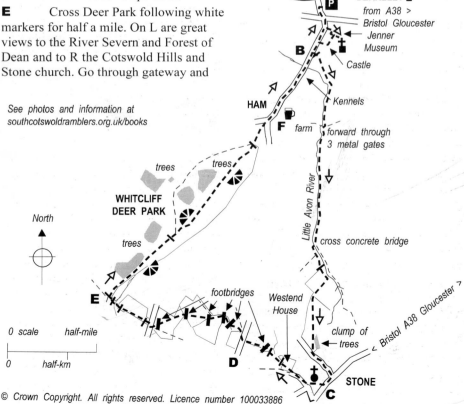

© Crown Copyright. All rights reserved. Licence number 100033886

25

An all seasons walk through hanging beechwoods, a fascinating quarry, and upper limestone grassland. Particularly attractive in early Spring when wood anemones and bluebells carpet the woodland floor, and in Summer when warblers are singing, and buzzards nesting in adjacent locations and seven orchid species growing along the way. Steep ascents but excellent views on a clear day.

Start: Park in Dursley May Lane CP (3 hour limit). From A38 into Dursley turn R at traffic lights into May Lane. From Stroud via Uley or from Tetbury go round the Market Hall roundabout,and swing L into Castle Street. Pass swimming pool on R and at next lights go forward into May Lane. In May Lane itself pass new library and bus station on R and car park entrance is just round next corner to R (Hill Road). **Maps:** Explorer 167, Landranger 162, grid ref. ST 754981.

Buses: Monday - Saturday only from Stroud and Stonehouse (20) hourly, from Gloucester (91) hourly, and from Bristol (309) 2 hourly to Dursley Bus Station in May Lane.

Food and Drink: The Old Spot Inn, May Lane, Dursley - 01453 542870, The New Inn, Waterley Bottom - 01453 543659 (do ring them first as occasionally closed).

A   On leaving car park turn R up the next part of May Lane (south) and continue to far end. Now turn L steeply up Hunger Hill and at far end turn R up a bridleway into woods. Keep to L track at junctions but continue to climb (avoid path going down to L). You will reach a semi-clearing. Bear R along main track. At bridleway crossroads by posts and chain go straight across to reach a road.

B   Continue L along road to a junction (signposted North Nibley), and after another 100 yards cross over stile on R. Now go straight ahead into Breakheart Quarry and turn R at a low footpath sign. Now circle to L within quarry area, noting floral surprises. Here you can obtain a view of the William Tyndale monument. Join access road and pass between Nuclear Electric buildings. Leave road where it swings to L and go forward past information board (Sunny Scrubland) and through trees to reach a stile. Cross this one, ignoring stile on R, and soon cross another into open area. Go in same direction (L of first electricity pole). There is a splendid view over

Waterley Bottom. Keep on to gate which comes into view in far corner.

C   Enter lane over fence next to gate and turn R down a steep winding woodland path to a stile. Go straight down field, and at end of fencing, turn L to reach a kissing gate under trees. Descend to road. You should emerge by the New Inn, Waterley Bottom. Go down to the junction and follow road sign L to Wotton-u-Edge. Go L again at the next junction towards Whiteway. Pass cottages and bear L opposite barn up to gate.

D   Head straight up field to a small gap in line of trees just to L of slight hump. Climb up passing coppiced trees and in 30 yards you should reach a stile. Now climb two flights of steps until you reach a wide track. Ignore steep path opposite and turn R along the track. Follow this through the woods as it gets steeper until it curves L up to gates. Go through kissing gate turning L on to road, and L again at fast main road (A4135). Walk **carefully** along L verge and at next junction cross over to walk downhill on R facing oncoming traffic. Round L bend you will spot an escape lane ahead. Just before the bend cross to L **with great care** and walk up escape lane / bridleway. Follow the bridleway over a vehicle barrier on a small track passing quarry on L. Climb up a little way and bear L through woods following occasional painted blue bridleway arrows, later converging towards level road on L.

E At timber posts turn R. Proceed down steeply winding sunken path (locally called Crooked Mustard) avoiding tracks off to L. At bottom of wood turn L on to track and continue for

200 yards. There are usually good views of Cam Peak and Long Down from here. Swing R to reach metalled road. At junction turn L up Nunnery Lane. Soon join a track up into wood. On entering the wood turn R along track near woodland edge (muddy in places). Go R at signpost down another sunken lane to a road - if visibility is good watch for surprise view of May Hill and the distant Malverns over Dursley Church. Go down beyond a row of cottages and turn L on paved path. This wiggles between hedges and fences and emerges at a junction. Go straight on across and cross another junction. Now continue along The Slade to reach May Lane and the car park. Over the road is the Old Spot Inn. Perhaps visit the town centre. The Market Hall and Parish Church are well worth seeing.

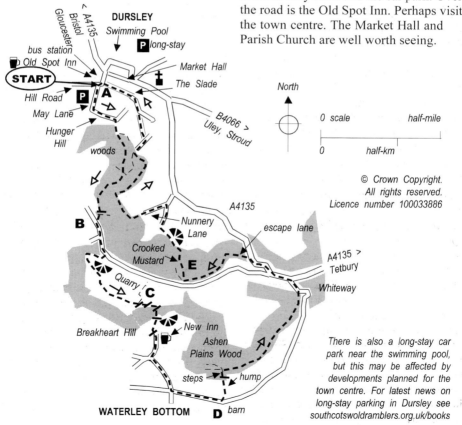

© Crown Copyright.
All rights reserved.
Licence number 100033886

There is also a long-stay car park near the swimming pool, but this may be affected by developments planned for the town centre. For latest news on long-stay parking in Dursley see southcotswoldramblers.org.uk/books

27

From Nailsworth you will pass along a deep valley containing many fish ponds with occasional herons until the walk reaches peaceful Horsley village. The return section on a higher route gives you wide views of Minchinhampton Common and Nailsworth. This is a short walk over moderate terrain, packed full of interest. Allow plenty of time, for, as one of Nailsworth's most illustrious residents, W.H.Davies, wrote, "What is this life, if full of care, we have no time to stand and stare." Afterwards you could mooch around Nailsworth's individualistic shops.

Start: Nailsworth is a bustling centre and can be busy at times. Try Newmarket Road Car Park, Nailsworth (23 hour limit) or further up the same road for some possible on-street parking, but do not block anyone's access (see map). Walk back towards the centre and start just past the Britannia Inn at the junction of Old Market and Market Street.

Maps: Explorer 168, Landranger 162, grid ref. ST 848995.

Buses: Monday - Saturday Stroud (46,93,40) every 30 mins, Cheltenham (46) & Gloucester (93) hourly, Wotton-under-Edge (40) 2 hourly. Sunday (46) Stroud/Cheltenham, six all day. Walk from bus station (toilets) to L along Old Market to start at junction with Market Street on L.

Food and Drink: Britannia Inn, Nailsworth - 01453 832501, Bell and Castle, Horsley - 01453 832155, Ruskin Mill Coffee Shop (vegetarian lunches / drinks 11-4 Tue-Sat) - 01453 837514.

A   At its junction with Old Market, turn along Market Street. Take first on R, Brewery Lane and after 50 yards fork L uphill on a surfaced footpath. Follow this ignoring L fork, and continue ahead to road, crossing carefully. Follow footpath opposite, and after 50 yards fork R. You reach Ruskin Mill (coffee shop here). Note undershot waterwheel and mill race. Keep L and go straight on beside large mill pond (sometimes drained). Keep on path near to pond as it climbs up steeply and down again to pass houses. Turn R down steps to cross footbridge.

B   **EITHER** On the L is the entrance to Ruskin Mill grounds with a wooden arched bridge, and it is a delight to walk through the grounds on one of the currently permissive paths up the valley passing the main building to reach a level drive.*(now see letter C)* **OR** The public footpath goes up steeply to steps to reach road near old toll house, Pike Cottage. Turn L along road until 100 yards after

Horsley sign, bear L down drive into the former fishery.

C   Pass ponds to reach a gate and stile. Leaving Ruskin Mill land you now enter Willow Fishery and walk past lakes and then Mill House. Bear L along enclosed path and through gate. Turn R past tall conifer hedge on R to reach a lane. Turn L with stream on L. Pass cottages on R to reach a road (Washpool), and go across. Continue along valley to junction of paths and go uphill a short way to the R, keeping stream and pond on L. Carry on along the level path to reach the road (Hartley Bridge), and then turn sharply R up the hill to reach the Bell and Castle in Horsley. **[Walk 14 might be followed from here, D]**

D   Go uphill past the Bell and Castle, Church and school on L. Cross here and look for a footpath signpost on R. Turn R along track which becomes a downhill footpath. After steps, go over stile and turn R through meadow and over

28

stile into lane in the hamlet of Downend. Go L along lane and follow round to R. At next junction look for concrete footpath marker to go up path ahead behind cottages. After next stile bear half R (see waymark) up meadow to go through gateway. Continue in same direction with fence on L to an old metal gate in corner. This has stone pillars. Go through and along top of next field to top L corner stile. Head across middle of next field keeping level. Just below top of far hedge go up a few steps to cross 2 stiles. Shortly cross high stile on L into paddock and head half L to another high stile out again into field. Continue up field to far corner with house and stone wall on R. Cross stile by stone slab and turn R along lane.

E Walk downhill past house called "Cleeves" to stone stile on R. Go diagonally down field to gap near corner. Continue in next small field to stile by gate, then keep L in next field to reach a stile down in corner. Cross and go down steps to track. Turn R down track to road. Cross over and go down another track to another road. Turn R for 20 yards, then bear L down surfaced path. Halfway down at cross paths continue down to reach Newmarket Road. Turn R past a chapel to reach car park or continue to bus station.

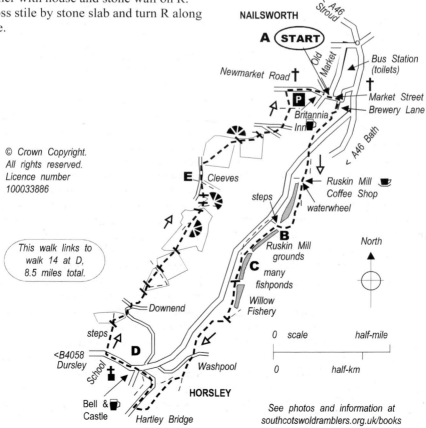

© Crown Copyright. All rights reserved. Licence number 100033886

This walk links to walk 14 at D, 8.5 miles total.

NAILSWORTH

A START

Newmarket Road

Bus Station (toilets)

Market Street

Brewery Lane

Old Market

< A46 Stroud

< A46 Bath

Britannia Inn

E Cleeves

steps

Ruskin Mill Coffee Shop

waterwheel

B
Ruskin Mill grounds

North

C many fishponds

Willow Fishery

Downend

steps

<B4058 Dursley

School

D

Washpool

HORSLEY

Bell & Castle

Hartley Bridge

0   scale   half-mile

0   half-km

See photos and information at southcotswoldramblers.org.uk/books

29

Walk 14   M   Kingscote and Horsley

5.5 miles / 9 km / 2 h 45 m

Heather Garner

There are extensive views over the Cotswolds before descending from sleepy Kingscote village through fields, deciduous woods and secretive valleys to Horsley. There are more delightful woods and fields up to Kingscote. In February see the aconites and snowdrops in Conygre Wood.

Start: Hunters Hall Inn car park, Kingscote on A4135 Dursley - Tetbury road, grid ref. ST 813960. Park in the side road opposite away from the corner or in Hunters Hall Inn car park only if you plan to patronise them. **Alternative Start:** Park tidily in Horsley village to start walking from the Bell and Castle, grid ref. ST 838980. If you start from Horsley you can shorten the walk by a mile. **Maps:** Explorer 168, Landranger 162. **Buses:** Monday - Saturday from Nailsworth, Stroud, Wotton-under Edge (40) 2 hourly. **Food and Drink:** Hunters Hall Inn, Kingscote - 01453 860393 or the Bell and Castle, Horsley - 01453 832155.

A From Hunters Hall Inn cross main road carefully, turn R to walk along verge, which soon becomes pleasantly wider, until you reach a bridleway sign on the L. Follow this enclosed path to its meeting with a footpath. Here turn L and follow field edge path with hedge on your L to a metal gate and gap. Continue to enter Kingscote churchyard. Through the churchyard keep the church on your R and walk to the Lych Gate.

B From Kingscote Church go downhill a few yards and then bear L along a lane signed no through road past cottages to reach a stone stile into a field. Keeping the boundary on your R, follow to an iron kissing gate. Continue following the hedge downhill until you reach a stile with marker post. Go down field to stony crossing of stream, and slightly R up the other side to a stile to the L of double metal gates. Go up field to cross a drive and stile by power line. Continue, aiming towards L hand bottom corner of wood. Cross a small stream and climb uphill with wood on your R to a stile up into it.

C The path runs through the wood for 400 yards to a stile into field. Go half R across field that is usually cropped, aiming to L of clump of trees, to reach a track. Continue in same direction across next field, also usually cropped. Aim for a prominent house on ridge, seen above a small wood in valley. A stile comes into view as you descend. Cross and go down in same direction skirting the trees to reach a footbridge and stile under pylon cables. Follow the path up through the wood to a track and lane. As the lane bends sharply L uphill, cross a stile on R and down a few steps into the field. Follow the barbed wire fence round on your L, keeping to high ground until you reach a stile in top corner just past small waterfall. Cross into a higher field and gradually bear L uphill, and half way across it Horsley Church tower should come into view. Go through metal kissing gate to cross to the far corner of playing field. At the other side with the church on your L, take a path L behind the houses, through a gate into the churchyard, and keep the church on your L. By main church door turn R to reach road through wrought iron gateway. Turn R along pavement to Bell and Castle, Horsley. **[Walk 13 might be followed from here, D]**

D **[Alternative Start]** From Bell and Castle, Horsley, cross over side road and

30

go downhill (Priory Fields Nos 1-4) and bear R onto lane (signed Bridlepath and Sandgrove). Follow this route down into Horsley Wood. At the bottom of the track, after it crosses a short embankment, bear L past a terrace of houses and through a gap by gate. Follow the track through the woods. Look for stream tumbling down on R. The track goes down through the woods, bearing L at bridleway sign (blue) to reach a usually muddy clearing. Turn L and follow footpath uphill. At three way parting of tracks, take the R path steeply up. Near top bear round L and a straight section brings you to a stile out of the wood.

E   Head half L up across field towards L of tree on skyline, until you reach a stile in far corner. Cross next field to reach a metal gate in far R corner.

Continue with hedge on your R to a gap. Go through and continue in same direction with hedge on L to reach a stile. Emerge onto road and go downhill past cottages on R to corner. *(On the L is a kissing gate into Conygre Wood, Kingscote, renowned for its snowdrops and aconites in February. If you decide to explore the wood, return to this kissing gate to continue the walk).* Turn R uphill to reach Kingscote Church. *(If you started the walk at Horsley and wish to take a short cut of a mile, continue now from letter B).* Walk up the road from the church to the corner, and turn L just before the telephone box and bus stop. Walk along the pavement to the main road and cross carefully over to Hunters Hall.

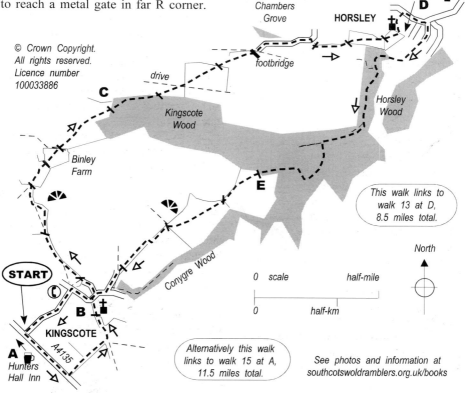

Bell & Castle Inn

D

Chambers Grove

HORSLEY

drive

footbridge

C

Kingscote Wood

Horsley Wood

Binley Farm

E

This walk links to walk 13 at D, 8.5 miles total.

North

START

Conygre Wood

0   scale   half-mile

0   half-km

B

KINGSCOTE

A

Hunters Hall Inn

A4135

Alternatively this walk links to walk 15 at A, 11.5 miles total.

See photos and information at southcotswoldramblers.org.uk/books

31

This part of the Cotswolds appears to be a level plateau, but several deep valleys, or "bottoms", are cut into it and this walk explores Ozleworth Bottom and the Bagpath Valley. Both are well-wooded, with few buildings and fewer people. This is real "Shangri-La" country!

Start: Hunters Hall Inn car park, Kingscote on A4135 Dursley - Tetbury road. Park in the side road opposite away from the corner or in Hunters Hall Inn car park only if you plan to patronise them. **Maps:** Explorer 167, Landranger 162, grid ref. ST 813960.

Buses: Monday - Saturday to Kingscote from Stroud, Nailsworth and Wotton-under-Edge (40) 2 hourly. **Food and Drink:** Hunters Hall Inn, Kingscote - 01453 860393.

A　From Hunters Hall Inn go along main road past car park entrance and outbuildings. Cross side road (signed Newington Bagpath), and go through kissing gate and along by field boundary on R. Follow track as it leads out of field down through trees and through gateway into an enclosed route. Go through metal gate into field and continue down L side to second metal gate. Here go ahead towards metal water trough in corner in Hay Bottom. Go through hand gate and cross footbridge. Continue uphill slightly L of footbridge angle (see waymark on bridge) to reach edge of field and carry on up steeply. At the end of field, go through gateway in R hand corner into a lane.

B　Pass through gap opposite into field which is usually cropped and continue ahead. Aim for L of a group of trees on the skyline if in any doubt. At far side, bear R at wall and follow it through gap on to Scrubbett's Lane. Turn R, passing a lane coming up on L, to crossroads. Here turn L and in 30 yards turn L again on to enclosed path. Go down this and through gate to see Bagpath Valley below you. Follow wall on L and then through waymarked gap. Then turn R going downhill between fence and trees past footpath sign on horse chestnut tree. Soon bear L down valley and eventually reach a fence. Pass through small gate on L. Continue downhill through two more gates with stream on your R. At the second gate there are in fact two. Take the L one. The one on the R goes up to the mansion in Ozleworth Park. Then on R pass a stone pillar and other remains of "London Bridge", so called because it was large and ornate, built in the 18th century.

C　Continue, keeping stream on your R down valley. Ignore track up on L. Look for small gate on R, beyond which is a ford. The footbridge on R is not our route. Cross ford and keep on the level to reach a track after several yards. *(If area is too wet see below.)* At track turn L over footbridge by second ford to gate and stile. Cross stile and the route is ahead. *(If first ford area proves to be too wet, return through small gate, turning sharp R through a wide gateway, and go on a permissive route through field to reach a clear track. Here turn L.)* Walk up good track with stream on R. Pass gate and stile into woods to follow footpath through Ozleworth Bottom. Eventually the wide track bears L and begins to climb steeply. After 20 yards uphill, turn R off track and keep level to Boxwell Lane, a track.

D　Opposite is a rather hidden old metal gate with stone pillars. Pass by them and walk up valley with a lake on your R. After crossing a footbridge by ford, the route passes another lake on L, then enters Lasborough Park at a gate. Go past mansion, which is up on L, to another gate by cattle grid. Follow track to cross drive and continue uphill in same direction (waymarked) to top of valley side. Near top bear R and contour around hillside, with views R to Lasborough Manor (part Tudor) and its attendant chapel. Lose height slightly and look out for small gate in stone wall. Beyond is a mound, which is the remains of a Norman "motte", or castle mound, surrounded by a ditch. Further on are some trees and a hidden building, a church no longer used. Before church turn R down field to reach a hidden gate. Turn L and go up the road.

E **[Alternative Start** - Just past old Newington Bagpath church on L is a grassy verge suitable for parking (grid

ref. ST 815948)]. After passing church on L bear R off the road through gateway with stone wall on your R. As wall bends round, path becomes a track into wood. Go along and then down - watch out for badger sett holes. Emerge into Hay Bottom through gate. Turn L along here towards distant water trough you passed earlier. Contour round hillside to metal gate up on R. Go through this and retrace your steps up to Hunters Hall Inn.

Hunters Hall Inn

A KINGSCOTE

START

North

A4135

water trough
footbridge
Hay Bottom

B

This walk links to walk 14 at A, 11.5 miles total.

Church Covert

E

P

motte

Newington Bagpath old church

Lasborough Manor

drive

Lasborough Park Mansion

woods

lake

OZLEWORTH BOTTOM

woods

D

footbridge / ford

lake

Boxwell Lane (stone pillars / gate)

C "London Bridge"

woods

sometimes marshy ford

footbridge / ford

0 scale   half-mile

0   half-km

BAGPATH

woods

See photos and information at southcotswoldramblers. org.uk/books

This walk is full of contrasts with views of Wotton-under-Edge from all directions. The route goes through the historic town (well worth exploring at some stage), then follows a meandering stream before a steep climb up Coombe Hill, with impressive views. It continues through lovely Conygre Wood and reaches the landmark trees on Wotton Hill, with a tremendous panoramic view. Later the walk levels out, before climbing back to Wotton.

Start: Five miles from junction 14 of M5. From Nailsworth take the B4058. Park in the well-signposted main car park in The Chipping (please note there are short and long stay sections).
Maps: Explorer 167, Landranger 162, grid ref. ST 755932. **Buses:** Monday - Saturday from Dursley & Bristol (309) 2 hourly, from Stroud & Nailsworth (40) 2 hourly or from Yate (627) hourly. **Food and Drink:** White Lion - 01453 842054, Falcon Inn - 01453 521005.

A   Leave the car park at the lowest corner along Rope Walk. Turn R down past the shops (Long Street), following it as it bends L into Church Street. Perhaps have a look at the Perry and Dawes Almshouses through the archway on the R (lovely stained glass window in chapel). Continue to junction by War Memorial and cross straight over to go past the Parish Church. Take the first R (Manor Lane). At the bottom, turn L along narrow path and after a few yards turn R into a factory yard. Cross this and go over a footbridge. Turn L on the path alongside the stream.

B   On meeting road turn R and follow Cotswold Way along the stream path. Upon reaching lane, turn R and immediately L, again following the stream, alongside a field and on to the lane. Turn L and then bear L along lane. As the lane bends up to the R at the end of houses go straight into field through small gate and follow L boundary to far corner. Turn R up field to corner and cross over stile to road. Perhaps sit on very old (1902) bench for a good view. Turn L along main road to corner.

C   Listen out as you cross over very carefully. Go up enclosed lane and after a few yards cross stile on R into field. Head up field, keeping old tree line on L, and climb up passing strip lynchets (ledges made by ancient ploughing) to stile in the top fence. Cross second stile and turn L, and after a short way bear R up a narrow path which climbs steadily around and up the hill. Where it opens out climb to electricity pole on skyline. Follow hedge on R to gate and stile. Continue through wood ignoring path down to L and where track bears R, fork L along footpath to reach Old London Road.

D   Turn sharp L downhill, and at L bend go up steps on R to a gate. Follow a delightful path through Conygre Wood. After a while you will pass a building up on R, and after a similar distance as path goes up a bit, look for stile and signpost on R to leave the wood. Turn L along road, and soon turn R up bridleway. At junction of paths, turn sharp L and follow Cotswold Way along field edge to a gate on the R. Walk down to the walled clump of trees on Wotton Hill (*first planted in 1815 in honour of the Battle of Waterloo*). After enjoying the wide views, circle L and look for Cotswold Way leaving the hill. Follow this down until you reach the main B4060. *You could short-cut back to the centre by turning L from here (see map).*

E   Carefully cross the road, then turn R for a few yards, and take the footpath L between the cottages (just after number 26). Turn R down road, then just before bollards go L. At the bottom of this path cross Bradley Green, following footpath sign for Bushford Bridge. Follow the L hand hedge to a stile, then cross the next field diagonally to a gate. Continue along boundary on R to a stile onto road. Turn L and walk down to the junction. Note the castellated creeper-clad former toll house.

F   [Walk 17 might be followed from here, C]. Cross road and follow farm drive opposite. This path goes over a stile by gate and along over stile into Hopyard farmyard. Go out through L gate on to

track. Continue via a series of gates/stiles. Nearing Kingswood, you should spot a stile to L of gate onto the Kingswood Road opposite large house.

G   [Walk 17 joins here] Turn R, then L into Vineyard Lane. After a quarter of a mile, as the lane turns R by houses, turn L onto a track. Go over stile into field and cross to stile and gate on far side. Continue across next field, keeping to the R of Haw Park Farm. Go over the next stile, keeping to the R of the field, and turn R over a stile, halfway up hill. Immediately turn L uphill, through a gap in the old hedge. Go straight across the next field and over a stile onto a wide grassy path near a school playing field. When you reach the road, opposite, up to the L, is the car park.

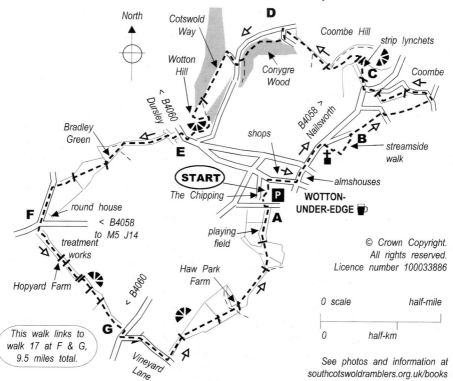

See photos and information at
southcotswoldramblers.org.uk/books

This walk links to walk 17 at F & G, 9.5 miles total.

Walk 17   L   Kingswood and Charfield Green
4.75 miles / 7.5 km / 2 h 15 m
John Corry

This is a reasonably level walk amongst the fields and streams of the southern Gloucestershire countryside starting from the village of Kingswood with the English Heritage Abbey Gatehouse site. It passes an old creeper covered round house and a most unusual and innovative new house, returning via the edge of Charfield village with panoramic views of Wotton-under-Edge and the Cotswold hills.

Start: 5 miles from M5 Junction 14 - well signposted. 10 miles from Nailsworth - take A46 then B4058. Park on The Chipping by Dinneywicks pub and Spar shop / post office. **Maps:** Explorer 167, Landranger 162, grid ref. ST 746917. **Buses:** Monday - Saturday from Dursley & Bristol (309) 2 hourly, from Yate (627) hourly. **Food and Drink:** The Spar shop sells supplies of food and drink. For a pub meal try the Fleece Inn, Hillesley - 01453 843189 (2 miles SE) or places in Wotton-under-Edge (see Walk 16) - as no food is served at the Kingswood pub.

A   From The Chipping, go down the High Street until you reach the Abbey Gateway. The Abbey Gatehouse is all that remains of a Cistercian Abbey after it was demolished by Henry VIII. The keys are available from the custodian at certain times (notice under the arch on R) if you would like to see inside. Now turn L along the street **just before** the Abbey Gatehouse to pass Kingswood Primary School. At main road go R to pass former Tubbs Lewis & Co (knicker elastic) mill (1854) on L. Pass Vineyard Lane on R. **[Walk 16 might be followed from here, G]**

B   Take footpath marked by a gate on the L, climb over the stile and follow the path keeping near to the hedge on your R. To the L is a converted textile mill and a small light industrial area. Continue over a stile and through a number of gates and a path between two hedges and through a farmyard to reach the Charfield to Wotton road.

C   **[Walk 16 joins here]** Here you will see an old round house on your R – this was probably used many years ago to collect tolls. Over the road cross a stile and follow the marked footpath towards a building on the horizon, to stile. Cross next field and go over a small bridge. The path across the next field is normally well marked through any crops; however if not, aim for large tree in middle of field and then take a slight angle to the L down to footbridge in R corner of field. Follow path up by Berry (Burrough) Hill Farm. Pass the farmhouse on your L and take track on R. Follow this track, which develops into a road after a short distance, until you reach a junction.

D   At the junction turn L up Swinhay Lane. Along this country lane you will pass on the L one of the most unusual new houses to be built anywhere in the country. This house was built for Sir David McMurtry, co-founder of the highly successful Renishaw Engineering Company (nine Queen's Awards to date). From here you can see in the distance one of Renishaw's properties – the converted New Mills. The walk continues along the quiet lane for about a mile. After going down and up again ignore first path (both sides of road) and after 150 yards look for a stile on the L. Here you turn sharply L to go along by the hedge on L to a gap. Now cross the next level field. The path across here is usually well marked to the stile in the distance. There are good views over the valley of the Little Avon River.

Over the stile head slightly L to the end of the hedge, where the path goes downhill. Aim for a stile to the L of the L hand metal gate ahead. Turn R and cross the bridge over the river. Continue to reach the start of a road. Take the footpath on the R across a small field and over a plank footbridge with stiles at each end. At this point the path is not that clear – go about 45° L up the slope of the field towards a small stile in a wire fence. Over the stile the path is again not very clear - walk R towards some large farm buildings just over the hill. Walk downhill near some buildings on the R towards a footpath sign in R corner of field. Cross over the road, **but beware,** it can be busy with the bends and fast traffic. Take the marked footpath just to the L by the small factory.

E Follow the footpath half L, which is usually very well marked through any crops, across two fields. After climbing over the stile in the second field you have Elbury Hill in front of you. Skirt round the hill to the L and just after the hill turn slightly L and through a gate. Follow the path up the hill to reach a drive which leads to Grange Farm. Cross this drive. In next field aim for gap to R of small copse. From here cross two more fields - aim for the stiles in each case. You will come to a gate and stile with a number of way markers – follow the one to the R. Again the path is not always clear – you are aiming for the top R hand corner of the field where there is stile and gate. Cross the next field and over a small stile, then over another field (which can be very muddy in winter) aiming for the L corner where there is a stile. Cross into an enclosed grassy path which takes you back to Kingswood near the shop and pub.

See photos and information at southcotswoldramblers.org.uk/books

This walk links to walk 16 at B & C, 9.5 miles total.

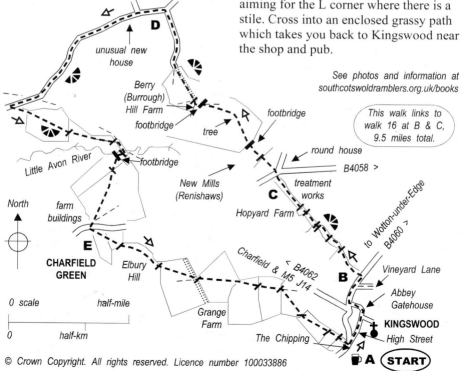

This is an open level walk across ancient fields with dry stone walls. The edge of Westonbirt Arboretum is reached before the route leads back to Leighterton. Numerous meadow birds including the rare corn buntings can be seen, and hares are often sighted on the grassy slopes near the end of the walk. For a small village, Leighterton has much to interest the visitor and the walk ends with a short tour. Not on the walk, but near to the school, trees mark the largest Neolithic Burial Chamber in the Cotswolds.

Start: Travel via the A46 (Bath to Stroud road). Three turnings off the A46 lead to Leighterton. The middle one leads past the school. Turn R at the next junction to park at (if planning to visit) or near the Royal Oak in Leighterton. **Maps:** Explorer 168, Landranger 162, grid ref. ST 823912. **Buses:** From Tetbury only (279) - one bus on Wednesdays and Fridays.

Food and Drink: The Royal Oak, Leighterton - 01666 890250 or within the Arboretum.

A   With your back to the Royal Oak main car park entrance (by large tree), turn R along road and at junction R again to pass a red post box on L. After 100 yards turn L onto footpath after a house called "The Cuillins". After crossing three wooden stiles by gates close together, follow the path diagonally across several fields surrounded by dry stone walls. Keep on course by checking back to previous stile at each crossing, and refer to map opposite. After a field adjacent to a group of barns, cross stile and follow the wall on your L to stiles. Now bear L to reach a drinking trough set in the stone wall opposite.

B   Cross the stile by the trough and climb half R to the top of the rise, when the next stile will be visible. Bear slightly R, but still go diagonally, to reach a gate near far end of R hand wall. The trees of Bowldown Wood are a useful guide. *(For the far sighted, Tetbury Spire in the distance is a good marker).* Go through the gate and cut across the corner of next field to another gate. Continue in same direction near the edge of the wood. Go through another gate and then in a similar direction to the road.

C   Turn R, walk on the wide verge to the crossroads in the dip. Turn R to continue along this minor road until a R bend is reached just before an uphill section. *(Those who wish to do so can follow the road back to Leighterton and point F).* The walk continues through the metal farm gate on the L. Follow the grassy track in the valley bottom with the field boundary on the R, eventually passing through a farm gate into a wood.

D   This track (sometimes very muddy) ends in a clearing where another track meets it from the R. *(The gate at this point leads you to a stile on the R into Westonbirt Arboretum, where you may choose to extend your walk. There is a shop and café there. If you decide to go there, return to this point to continue this walk).* The walk now turns R along the track through the wood westwards towards Leighterton. Do not be tempted along side tracks, but go through a farm gate and ahead on a grassy route between a wall on the L and ancient small trees on the R. Reach a wooden stile on the R of a metal gate.

E   Cross the stile and go half R up the slope. At the top of the rise take care to aim for the jutting angle of the wall and continue keeping this wall on your R *(see map)*. Cross a stile. Further on go over another stile near a farm gate and continue with wall on R to a stone stile in the wall. Cross and head gradually away from wall towards a distant metal gate near the village onto the lane. At gate, go straight on along the lane into the village. Look out for the small cemetery on the R, where you may find the time to spend a moment. *Part contains well-tended graves of young Australian Flying Corps airmen from a nearby airfield who died during the 1914-18 war and some sadly in training in 1919. There is a memorial stone here dedicated by the Prince of Wales in 1994. The airmen are also remembered in the village church which you may wish to visit a little later.*

F   Continue along the lane and turn L at The Mead to take a short tour of the village *(you could short cut back to the Royal Oak by keeping straight on)*. Pass a minute Chapel with 'Dolls House' porch and then the 13th century Church, which has an incongruous half-timbered tower: an economy measure when the Victorians ran out of cash and could not afford to replace the original castellated tower. Turn L at the next junction, passing mellow Cotswold houses to reach the village duck pond with its noisy inhabitants. Go R at cross roads (signed Bath Road) and then R at T-junction. Pass Church Farm Barn (1733), which is now converted to a dwelling house amidst the building development, but happily still retaining a huge pigeon loft and dovecote. Continue back to the Royal Oak.

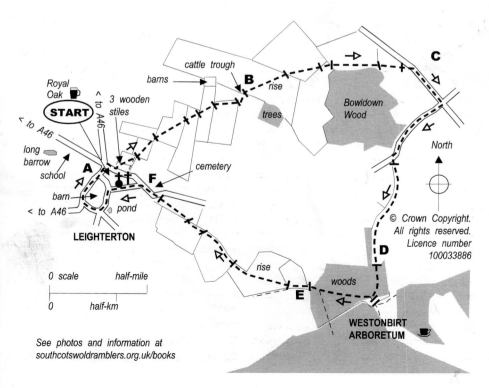

See photos and information at southcotswoldramblers.org.uk/books

Index to Book One Walks

KEY to the ups and downs on each walk

L	Level or little climbing
M	Moderate mix of hilly and level paths
M/H	Moderate to Hilly - more hilly than M
H	Hilly ups and downs most of the time